I0491112

Know The Buyer
Close The Sale!

Written By:
Kyle Newton

Added Notes by:
Colton Boudreau

Preface:

Hey reader, before you continue, allow me to tell you what this book's intentions are. This book can't promise you'll rise to #1 in the field of your choice. However, it will reveal the secrets that can put you ahead of your competition in learning how to sell, saving months of *your* time! And that means saving *a lot* of money. By cultivating the skills in this book, you'll find it's all you need to be successful in growing your bank account every week. This book is a beginner's guide to discovering the mental process of those you're selling to, and how to meet them on their energy level to help sinch the deal. You'll also notice more comfort in 'closing' your deals.

Allow me to tell you a little about myself: I am a self-published author who has spent 10 years in figuring out how to master sales and stay one step ahead of bigger publishers. And if your 'will' is ready, you'll find resources you never thought of. This book might one of them, especially if you are just looking into how to close deals and sales. Social media is a beast that deserves its own book. And as important as social media is, needing to close a deal can be just as or even *more* important. Stay tuned for my book on social media coming soon.
When I had my first book published, I didn't have a job, so I learned the importance of closing quickly. For almost a year, I was knocking on every

door to every business in New England, hoping they would put my novel on their shelf. Bookstore, to café, to a train station(The one in North Conway, New Hampshire), I didn't care. If they had a shelf with space to sell, I had a product to fill it with. At first, my sale's pitch was damaging and self-inflicting. The worst part is—I didn't even know it! Sometimes, it was decent. Other times, it was a damn train wreck(yes, particularly at the station I tried to sell at). But as time went on, I sharpened my "elevator pitch" until it became muscle memory to relay it to anyone at anytime. This book is to help build that pitch. It'll also sharpen what knowledge you have by revealing how to interact with different styles of buyers, both emotional and logical shoppers. (I also like how this book explains ways of being a saleman without being a 'Snake-Oil' Salesman, but that's just a personal prefrence.)

Going back to my auhor-becoming-saleman story, I found a store that not only took one or two books, but wanted me to *SELL THERE* once a week. With that being my only job, I needed to make sure I sold my book to anyone interested and to move those uninterested out of my way(or find a way to make them interested).

Time had never seemed more important. Everyday I drove to the store to sell my book, I had that fusion of excitement and nerves, forcing me to use my time to its fullest! This book holds the secrets that I learned that year (through a rather tough trial and error period), and the successes that followed in the oncoming years.. From how to come off as confident, even if you aren't too sure of yourself, to my techniques I used to build and sell the series Penny Punkers! If you want to find a way to be charismatic to customers and investors, keep reading!

A Quick Note On Muscle Memory Magnetism(Charisma)

Confidence is everything when it comes to selling. Anyone reading this find their palms a little sweaty when there's dozens of eyes staring at you? What if there was a way to control the energy of that room and find the ability to guide it? Once you discover how to read your customer, selling becomes much easier. It becomes so easy, one-on-one or to a crowd, you'll always be able to find a way to bring *their* energy to *your* comfort level.

Excluding the first statement of the previous paragraph, this book won't be a 'confidence is what you need, it's what we *all* need, I need you to believe like Tony Robbins!' page after page junk pile. I'm so tired of hearing that. Of course confidence helps you get what you need! It's called *confidence* for a reason! So, rather than us searching for confidence, how about we bring confidence to us? Yeah, we like the sound of that, too.

Figuring out where someone is on their emotional scale, changing their mental state, and then getting *the buyer* interested in being sold on your deal. Isn't that what you *really* want? Sales are great, don't get me wrong. But to be inside the mind of your customer (or possible investor) before they even open their mouth to speak? You'll be miles ahead of them in the conversation!

When you sell, you need to sound as though you are 200% confident about what you are saying. Speak with certainty and everyone will believe you. If you don't, your audience will see that immediately and never trust you. Always remember: an audience of one or one million **WANTS** to learn or "be bought" on what you're selling. So they are looking for reasons to believe you and trust you. If you start stumbling over your words or using "um," "you know," "uhh," or any other "space fillers," when you haven't strategically planned it, they'll start to doubt you and you'll immediately lose your sale. You've got about 3-5 seconds to capture your audience. So in that short amount of time, remember to greet them with a proud attitude and act like you know exactly why you're there(because you should already). Do that, and anyone with even the slightest interest in being sold will respond!

Elevator Pitch

For many of you reading, I'm sure you've heard of this. If so, skip to the next part.

For those who don't know, allow me to explain. Your "elevator pitch," is your 20 second sales pitch for your product. You need to pretend you've just stepped into an elevator alongside Robert Herjavec or Kevin O'Leary(or pretend it's both to really get your heart pumping) and you now have 20 seconds to tell them why *they* should be fighting each other for *your* product. What are the right verbal cues to get them to react the way *you* want them to and buy your product or idea?

Make sure it's long enough to be informative but not long enough to bore them, you don't need the whole 20 seconds. Which sounds better: (A) How would you like a phone that can specialize in stocks and stock-market news, or (B) Do you feel like you aren't accomplishing enough in your stocks? Or are you trying to get interested in stocks? Well not only can you take this phone with its stocks-info on the go, you can download apps that handles your finances, perform day-trades, and even let you know when your kids are home!

The second sentence, although slightly longer, is far more effective. It gives you a glimpse into what the product(in this case, the phone) can do, and gives enough interest to draw you in. It also has a slight joke to bring a sense of humanity from salesman & buyer. Make sure you establish that first and foremost! Step in and call the person by their first name, throw the Mr. and Mrs stuff away! Doing that often times disarms them. This isn't so much a trick, and more of a fact that people nowadays want to feel like they are a person, on 'a target,' and that'sfair. You don't want to feel like you're being hustled, do you? Yeah, didn't think so. That's why you should treat them like people: buyers are so ready to become defense, that it's almost a natural state for shoppers. Give them reason not to put that extra hurdle up, or better yet, let that niceness convince *them* to lower the defences.

Make your elevator pitch like a pin to a grenade: short, yet has enough power to command everyone's attention. Remember that you have 20 seconds. In the world of sales, that could be a few lifetimes!

Why Should You Even Bother With This Book Anyway?

Alright, now that we've spoken about charisma, confidence, and your elevator pitch, let's get to the meat of this book. As I said in the beginning, these 'Sales Hacks' were made when I had no income, one self-published book, and I was selling at a store that wasn't even a bookstore. In fact, it specialized in incense and witchcraft supplies! The owner allowed me to go down there and sell one day a week. Looking back on it now, I suppose the strategy of this sales-technique started even earlier than that.

I remember the weeks leading up to my first sale in that store (which is no longer open but was found in the small gem of a town called North Conway, found in northern New Hampshire). I was knocking on every bookstore's door, asking them if they would take a copy or two of my book. Sometimes, I would get them to take one. The rarity of selling two books ranks up there with that of a 1st Editon hologam Charizard Pokemon card (needless to say, I almost never had this happen. Other times, which was the commanding percentage of my attempts, ended up in me walking away without a single sale. I suppose this is partly due to the fact that my elevator pitch was filled with so many pauses that followed an "uhh" or "um," that most of the bookstore managers forgot why I was even there!

For those reading this who have self-published a book, an album, or any product you've personally created, you know about the promotion and money needed to get it seen and heard from the masses. My version of wanting to be seen and heard was to use the last of my money and order several copies of my books. And that was about the time the needle in my car was crawling so close to the letter "E" that I was contemplating on reaching into the dash and holding it in place for as long as possible. But, the gamble I placed on my dream was about to pay off...

I woke up one spring morning and decided that day would be the last day I'd attempt to sell my book before I went in search of a 9-5 job(which just saying those words still makes my skin crawl). I also decided that if that was to be my last day, I'd pour every ounce of confidence I could muster into my pitch. Literally, leave it '*all out there.*' Take note that you should learn from my mistake and pretend every pitch is your last, because you never know when you might be able to make your next sale. Or which one just needs that little extra push.

Even with my new resolve, I was getting shut down more than I had been any other day prior. I hadn't sold one book all morning. So after a quick lunch break of drinking tears and swallowing pride(and I believe a biscotti), I had run out of bookstores and started selling to other businesses. I still remember climbing up the stairs of the Luna Gallery and stared up at their 'open' sign with a drawn black cat thinking, "I'll give my pitch to the store owner, in hopes there's a desperate mother in there, looking for a last-minute gift. Maybe she'll hear my pitch?"

So I walked in there, revealed my book, and said "Hi, my name is Kyle Newton. How's it goin'? I'm a local author who has recently published a fantasy novel. I was wondering if you'd be interested in taking a copy to display on your shelves and possibly sell more should this one be bought from your store."

I'll never forget watching the only three employees staring at each other for what appeared to be several minutes(but were actually mere seconds). They then turned to me with wide eyes and said "You're a local author? That's incredible! Get the rest of your books in here and we'll set up a booth for you!"

Before I knew what was happening, the three employees had set up a table, a stand, and I heard them telling every customer in their "Mom & Pop" style shop, "Don't forget to buy a new book from local author Kyle Newton."

Up to that point, I thought selling one or two books to the local incense shop was going to be the most interesting sale overall. Come to find out my world had only gotten more interesting! I now had to sell my books to every customer who walked by. This made me feel much better about the chances of boosting my sales.

For a few weeks, I struggled to sell five a day. But through trial and error, I discovered a secret in how to understand the customer's shopping style. I eventually discovered a way to sell five times what I was selling before! Now, I live in a train caboose that's a micro-home, still writing and selling the same way I used to. Only now, I don't need to worry about a side-job.

Should you continue reading, you will be able to break down and understand how customers think/react when they shop or buy. It's the same technique I used and practiced while selling in that store. And perfected across New England to Stockhold!

The section of this book talks about the three "types" of buyers. The "Seers," the "Listeners," and the "Touchers." If you only read the next section of the book, should you apply it, you'll see a tremendous rise in your sales! So go forth, read on, and get those sales!

Trading With Touchers

Out of "Seers," "Listeners," and "Touchers," the "Touchers" are the easiest to sell to. At first, it may not appear this way because they tend to reach for the product before you can hand it over, which tends to make salespeople a little nervous. Again though, with a little bit of confidence, the 'Touchers' begin asking questions or make comments before you can get your first answer out. This is the best thing that could happen to you. It's took me sometime before I realized they weren't trying to be overwhelming, they *wanted* to buy the product already. They just didn't know it yet!

When I first started selling my books, this group of buyers made me nervous every time they stepped up. And to you, new salesperson, they may strike you as the more difficult class of buyer due to how quickly they get into your space and tend not to leave for a time. Nothing quite fills a salesperson's stomach with knots like someone stepping up to you, reaching and pulling at your display until you're so off balance you have no idea where you are in your pitch—which is the worst place to be! Then, once they have the product of yours that they want, they rain down with a barrage of questions, which half of them aren't even related to the product.

Without realizing it, they're trying to take control of the conversation and I was allowing it. *Hot tip: DON'T DO THAT!** Rapport comes from asking questions, which is what they're doing *for* you.

HOWEVER, it's not letting the customer tell you about how well they mow the lawn. Write that down if you must, because it took sometime before I got used to that concept and discovered that "Touchers," are not only quick to show their interest, but they do most of the work in closing the deal for you!

This next statement is not meant to offend anyone who picks this book up and discovers they are a "Toucher," but it's an easy way to state it. This is the group of buyers who are attracted to "shiny objects." They WANT a reason to buy the product you are selling. And this reason could be a number of things, which I will discuss later in the "7 Personalities" section of the book. However, their questions will often elude to what they want, making your job at figuring them out *way* easier than the other two buyer types.

When you find out what they want-focus on it! If your buyer(s) are attracted to one particular advantage your product offers, don't try to sell them on anything but that one advantage unless it benefits that single perk! You want to promote the focus they have on your product by propping it up(but don't glorify it!!! Remember, your buyers are people too, they don't want to feel like you're treating them as though they're simpletons. Their excitement will often hit a peak and you'll see where that plateau is as you continue your talk with them. Once they hit that peak, that is when you want to start talking about other perks to your product that compliment the one they are attracted to. That is usually enough to seal the deal on a sale. I have successfully sold my products to more "Touchers" than any other of the classifications of buyers, but you will soon do the same. Eventually you'll place each personality trait with a stage in where your customer is mentally on their readiness to buy.

A professor in the college I attended, once told me: "If you can present your product to the customer by using both hands, you'll drastically improve your chances of a sale."

He wasn't being sarcastic or dramatic. If you have a tangible product, hand it to your next customer with both hands and see how more willing they are to listen to you. You'll see a small bump in sales on that alone. This is because you appear to be more genuine. Try this test with a friend/spouse practice the action. It might feel strange at first, but that's normally. Instead of pointing out how awkward the first time can be, watch your friend's reception change. You'll notice their character 'warms' up to your pitch.

As you practice this action more, you'll notice you can't help but put your entire body into this action. That shows your care for your product as well as showing a care for the customer in focusing solely on them. This is a prime way to sell to this particular type of buyer. Use it for all, but you'll see the biggest boost here.

*A quick note on what I said above about "glorifying" your product. The best way to see an increase in sales is to hype up what you have. However, that doesn't mean lying about it. Those are two separate things all together. And the last thing you want to do is lie about your product. Especially, if you are within earshot of the next type of buyer we are going to discuss!

Leverage Against Listeners

As stated in the last section, I DO NOT encourage lying to your customers. If you're a good enough salesperson, you won't need to lie. There's nothing worse than lying and then being caught in your lie. The now *former* customers will tell those who *would've* been customers, and eventually no one will want to buy from you. This is what is known as "career suicide."

I bring this up because "Listeners" are the ones who are more likely to catch you in your lie than any other group. Where "Touchers" are already interested in your product and it's just up to you to keep them excited as you seal the deal, "Listeners" are in search of something to be interested in. In my experience, where "Touchers" practically encourage you about your own product by dwelling on it themselves, "Listeners" are people who may glance down at what your selling, they might even ask a few questions to get the conversation started, but it is mostly up to you to carry the conversation.

Your *genuine* hype will be what sells this product to this customer, so long as you know *why* they want it. This is where your confidence is needed AND tested. If you're nervous, remember to speak proudly, even if you're feeling intimidated. Never forget, buyers *want* to be sold on your product. *They want* to hear you be successful. That way, they can say they have a successful product. So, give them what they want and answer their questions to the fullest of your ability, and in return, they'll show appreciation by buying what you're selling! Now keep going and we'll wrap up this section of the book with the third and final type of buyer.

Selling to Seers

The third and final class of buyer is the most difficult to sell, to in my personal experience. If there is ever a time or place your charisma needs to shine, it's here (hopefully you've been practicing and honing your charisma already. Remember: Charisma isn't a gift as much as it is an art. Practice, and you'll be as charismatic as any motivational speaker out there).

The "Seers" are the class of buyers who will be staring at YOU, not the product. They will be expecting *you* to sell them on yourself. A book, a phone, gummy bears, or even a laser pistol. They won't even think of buying what you have if you are not 100% certain about the product. If a "Seer" asks questions-good! And if they look at your product(s) or pick it up-even better! (And we'll talk more about the importance of this in just a few minutes)They're going to keep asking questions, but you had practice answering anything they may ask due to your last customer who was a "Listener." So keep answering those questions, and remember: you're in control.

My old high school basketball coach used to tell me: "If things are moving too quickly, reset the pace. Slowing things down can help you regain control." Just like a basketball game, slow the conversation down if you start to feel rushed. After they ask a question, feel free to take a deep breath and begin with "Well, you see," or "Great question." When you do or say something, you're setting the tone. If you speak confidently/proudly about your product, they will see that, but if you aren't sure they'll notice your slouch, your lack of knowledge, and ultimatily, your lack of charisma.

When I first started selling my book, a salesman from a New York publishing company approached me. He stated he does what I was doing on a far larger scale and want to help me improve my pitch. I kindly accept his offer and began my elevator pitch. He began his (difficult) questions, and some were very unusual, such as: "Why is your book a fantasy?" and "Do you think it might be more successful as a science-fiction novel?"

I'd be lying if I told you those questions didn't unnerve me at the time. However, by the end, he walked away with a copy of my book in his hands! And here's why. When we were discussing my book, I noticed he picked it up and began flipping through the pages. He was holding it-He had done the hardest part himself!

Once he had it in his hand, I went in for the kill. I sang praises of my book, all while he continued to quiz and question me about if he'd be interested. After using skills from the "seven characteristics category," (he had a pride characteristic, which I will talk about more in that section) he soon paid me and walked on out with my book in hand, and my bank account slightly bigger. The best part? My confidence had never been higher.

That is when I learned another important rule for dealing with any type of personality. If you want your bank account to grow, don't fear questions. Train your brain to register questions as a good thing! The more questions they ask, the more interested they are. So maintain your confident appearance, keep that charisma flowing and control the pace. Then, wrap up your elevator pitch, get them interested, seal the deal, and watch your earnings grow.

A Final Note on the Three Types of People

Whether you've just begun selling or you're Barbara Corcoran herself (if you are, hey-big fan), I'm sure you know by now that no one person is strictly any of the three personalities mentioned above. Almost everyone will have a combination of all three. Some people might show one or two predominating traits, but as you practice looking at people in these three categories, you'll find that one stands above the others.

Finding out which of the three personalities is a person's dominating trait may actually be noticeable early on in conversation. Often times their tell is in how they respond. People who are interested in your product want to understand how it functions, or why it was created. And when someone wishes to learn, they'll want to learn in the easiest and fastest way that comes to them. That is when a person's subconscious reveals itself. As you ask the questions to understand the point of sale from your customer, watch how they physically interact for any signs of their dominate trait.

Keep an ear out for "Seers" by listening for sayings such as "I *see* how that could be helpful" or "I *see* what you are saying." Of course you can't "*see*" what people are saying and you certainly can't see the words coming from their mouths. But in their struggle to obtain the knowledge you're offering about the product, the more they want to learn (as long as you remain charismatic). That is when their style of learning is revealed in their attempt to gather an understanding. And if you are speaking to a "Listener" they'll most likely admit their understanding through phrases that involve the phrases such as "I *hear* that," or simply "I am *listening*."

"Touchers" are often caught using verbs that involve touching and holding such as "I'm *picking up* what you're *putting down*," "I get that" or "I can *wrap* my brain around that." It's about physically grappling with the understanding.

These are just some examples of what you might hear when selling. There are many more. And be sure to pay attention to other cultures. Selling to locals is a great first step in practicing to break down people into the three categories. It's when you step out of that comfort zone where you learn how to deal with other slang and phrases. And my hope is that the next section of this book will help you even more!

The Seven Characteristics

So, you've stepped out into the world, you've been practicing on organizers buyers into their three types, and you're still hungry for more? Good! Being a strong sales person of any kind means always being hungry for more sales. You deserve a HUGE congratulations for staying hungry!

That being said; never, in this book or in person, will I say my strategy guarentes a 100% success rate. Anyone who tells you that is a moron and deserves to step on a lego with their barefoot. I say that because there's no such theing as 'the perfect pitch,' because you can't sell everyone on one thing. You only have improvable pitches, so don't stop learning with this book. It's not the cure-all, but it can certainly benefit you.

More likely than not, you are going to have far more people say no than yes when you start. However, with time and practice, this technique can help boost your numbers (and your bank account with that!)

Very similar to the three types of people, this next section is an even deeper dissection of your buyer's interest. From here on out, I won't be talking about who comes to buy your product, but *why* they'll want your product.

What is This Technique About?

A few years ago, back when my lovely wife was only my 'just dating' girlfriend, I told her and a few it was 'the 3/7 technqiue.' She laughed at me so hard, the first edition of this book is under a pen name (no seriously, look up ' 3/7 Technique by Carrol N. Cote.' DO NOT BUY IT! It's the earlier version of this and proof I was nervous about this book's initial success. It's 5 Star rating quickly evaporated those fears.)

I won't spend hour sitting here thinking about some cool awesome Terminator styled name for this business strategy. All it is is this: Which type of buyer are you dealing with, why are they here? That's what this book can help you solve. Maybe when the 3rd edition pops up, it'll have a name, but right now the important part is that your pitch is improved. Who cares what it's called if it's helpful?

When To Be Weary of Wrath?

I put this one first because the core of its lesson is an excellent skill to employ on all the traits you come across, no matter the type of sale. Up to this point, we've spoken about all three 'buyers personalities' you'll interact with in sales. What we haven't spoken of yet are 'buyers intentions'.

Buyer's intention is the *why* to your buyer being ate your place of sales. Know the *why* of your buyer and your chances of sealing your deal rise exponentinally. The only thing probably more important than knowing the *why* of your buyer, is knowing how to build a line of trust with your buyer. I say that because it's still common thought that most independant salespeople are "swindlers," or "con-artist."

There isn't much you can do about their initial thought of you, but with a few tricks, you can get around that barrier and better your chances at opening a line of friendly communication with them. And if you can build a friendly relationship with your client, you can build a lifelong buyer.

Thankfully the customers that talk down to you or believe you're selling 'snake-oil,' are becoming less frequent when compared to today's average buyer. That being said, I bet on the occasion those doubtful-buyers approach you, they still make you cringe inside, right? That's okay, as a salesman, someties anxiety is a good thing.

Want to know how to defuse the anxiety in both you *and* the buyer, at least for the moment they're around? Change the atmosphere. By changing the atmosphere, I mean get them to lose the idea you're out to 'shake 'em down' for all the money in their purse/wallet. Instead, lower your energy to match their's. Start mimicking speech patterns and perform mirroring techniques to match their posture. Subconsciously, this will make your buyer feel comfortable around you without them even realizing it! This is because you've now affected their subconscious. You cause them to think *'they stand like me,'* or *'they laugh at what I laugh at.'*

You want these personal attachments. It strengthens your connection with your buyer. Perform these actions and they'll show signs of opening up. As they lower their guard, slowly bring the energy level up to your comfort zone and retake the sale. Another good way to look at this or study this is to use the pace, pace, lead technique!

Encourage The Envy

There's an easy trick to tell if a buyer is driven by envy: does this person still partake in Black Friday? It's 2020. If you feel you need to be part of the chaotic adrenaline-driven buying and not realize you can buy those items cheaper in October than on Black Friday(or online) then expect people to sell to your emotional blindless. When I say blindness, I mean being aware of the aggressive history that has befallen Black Friday in the last decade. From deaths to broken limbs, it's very serious, and COMPLETELY unneeded. However, business owners aren't stupid. If people are willing to buy, they're willing to sell. That's the beauty of a capitalist market: when you want, you get. That being said...

Buyers driven buy envy are emotional buyers. More likely to be Touchers' than most other traits, buyers associated with envy simply means they are emotion-driven buyers. Back in the 80's this was the person who was stereotyped as buying from CVS because 'they *thought* you'd love it.' Or the difficult family member who thinks 'you *should* love' what they bought you.

Don't let your guard down with they eager buyers though! Like anyone else, they want to know they are being treated like a person: not just a cash sign. And the dangers of upsetting this form of buyer could cost you dearly. Like I said before, these buyers are more likely to be at Black Friday over than other buyer. That means they know what's 'in' and have a lot of friends who probably do the same. This is what makes them one of your most common buyers. So, I'll end this chapter with a simple question: Do you want the most common buyer to be on your side or not? If the answer is yes, keep reading.

Separate From Sloth

This chapter is about the type of buyer trait that is most likely standing at the opposite side of the spectrum to the buyer driven by envy.

A sloth-styled buyer is a very casual buyer. This is the person who is often seen hanging out at the mall 'just because,' or your friend who likes to try clothes on, even though they won't buy anything. Many people see these buyers as indecisive, or very picky. You can look at it this way, but I choose to look at it as: this buyer knows their style/wardrobe/identity and are willing to wait to find that thing that's perfect to them.

Being a millenial, I will also use the example: Think of your friend who is really into anime. We all have one. And you now what I'm talking about: the type of anime fan who is so consumed with this style of cartoon, their notebooks and IG profiles are anime versions of themselves. Think about how dedicated this friend of yours is to any series you've heard them talk about. It's almost on par with someone from Boston being a Red Sox fan(which is also a good example). These people won't buy anything that isn't true to thr anime series, and fights viciously to enforce what's 'Canoonical.'

Search for the small group of people that treat your company like your friend defends anime. There may not be a lot of people that watch 'FullMetal Alchemist,' but those that prefer 'FullMetal Alchemist: Brotherhood,' are very vocal about it. If you don't believe me,type those two titles into Reddit and get back to us. No seriously, go and do it, we'll wait.

Welcome back! Freaking crazy right? Nothing says dedicated fanbase like 'I'll stab anyone who disagrees,' am I right?

Say what you will about such loyalty, but it says a lot about the product for people to be so dedicated to it. Perhaps you should treat your company or product with similar style? To be so genuine, or to craft something so reliable that people's pure dedication is promotion alone goes a long way for a long time. This is what 'Sloth-styled' buyers can offer you. They might not be anywhere near as numerours as those who shop through emotion like in the last chapter, this group is very small, but highly dedicated. It doesn't matter what the hottest new anime is, if a fan has a favorite, they tend to stay there. That means they are already connected to like-minded thinkers, which means like-minded buyers. Get one member of a dedicated fanbase to review your product, and watch your royalties rise!

Side Note When you work in sales, if you don't have some sort of script you've either remembered before stepping out onto your sale's floor, whatever that may be, or you keep a script in front of you during phone sales(which you better keep handy if you do over the phone sales), or you're already dead. And on top of that, if you don't guide your customer to your desired outcome, you are leaving far too many things to chance and you run the risk of losing the sale!

I'm going to state now that this information I'm offering can be used without acting like some sort of blood-thirsty shark. Every trick you will learn in this book will be taught how to make a sale without draining people of money and instead, making a slight rapport with them while they don't even realize it. Allow me to show you an example.

When I first started selling my books, I went door to door asking the question "Would you like to hear about my book?"

Ask that question out loud to yourself and listen to how I just gave a possible sale all the power in the conversation. They can say no, turn away, close the door, and never look back at me sulking in the rain as I blame them for not knowing good taste when it pounded on their door twenty seconds ago. Before I went blaming them for not appreciating greatness, how about I blame me for doing the same thing? You need to show your customer that your product will somehow improve their life

After my seventh or eighth attempt with this failed pitch, I was getting tired of hearing the sound of doors closing in my face. That's when store clerk number nine told me to ask the next store "a question that guides the sale, not ends it." After ten minutes or so of his kind time, we had the question I planned to ask the next few stores I visited. "Hey there, my name is Kyle Newton, I'm a local author selling my recently published fantasy book. How many copies would you like?"

Compare that question to "Would you like to buy my fantasy book?" See the difference already? I didn't give the option for the customer to back out and say 'no'. A lot of people consider this trick to be dastardly and underhanded. And to that I say it is, *only,* when you persist after the person declines you a second time. This book will help you get a sale from anyone who might be open to the possibility of a sale, not "how to make the impossible sale every time."

Before we continue, write down "Hey there, my name is (fill in), I'm selling (fill in). How many would you like?" Now, expand from here to perfect your new 20 second elevatpr pitch. Compare this pitch to your previous one and see how the two appear against one another.

Guided by Gluttony and Greed

These two are so similar I thought it was befitting enough to put them in the same chapter. Both in how to approach these buyers, and understanding these can be some of the friendliest/most dedicated fanbase to your product. Both traits deserve independant acknowledgement, but they have so many commonalities, it would be pointless to repeat information in two separate chapters.

Greed is the trickier beast to master, so we'll start here first. Someone who is seen as a 'greedy buyer' often generates the idea in people's mind as someone who steps on others to get what they want. Same for gluttony, leaving an impression that one must become so consumed with what they want they either don't care or have become oblivious to the fact they are hurting others to obtain what they are after.

Now that I have stated the obvious, darker side of the greed/gluttony in the buyer's world, let me say; those aren't the kinds of buyers we're focused on in this book. You are going to come across *SO* many people looking to buy your product. Whether they buy your product or not is the focus, not how many corrupt Wall Street Bankers you'll come across selling to (Because let's be honest, the chances of you selling to them are slim, much less crossing their path.) This book is going to introduce the more common, tamer version of these buyers.

Those who resemble more 'Greed' traits when buying will reveal themselves as passionate people. Whether they're on some sort of personal journey to acquire knowledge, a job, or some sort of benefit, they are dedicated to their 'wants'. If you're charismatic enough to create rapport with them, then there's a good chance the 'greed-based buyers' will reveal why they NEED what it is that you have. If they do this-capitalize on it! And no, I don't mean jack up the prices. In this fast-paced world, the last thing you want is to be seen as a scammer. Instead, make this customer feel welcome, but also fortunate in the fact they found you. Make them feel as though you're a special or secret tool out to personally aid them in their search for what they're after.

Remember, this book was written to help build and understand your customer's subconscious and in the same process boost your income. So if you can find out you should categorized the current customer as "greed-driven" and you can figure out which of the three personality types they are-use it! Convince them to check in frequently because your products are better. This may sound basic, but this type of deal does little for those who appear more "Sloth-like". Unlike other buyers, 'greed-based' clients *want* to know when the next product is coming out. That way, they have 'the collection.' Someone more 'sloth'oriented won't care about a collection, unless it *really* benefits them. And yes,that means altering your sales pitch to include the collection aspect in these sales. It's difficult to alter your pitch on the fly, *at first*, but to do so for these customers could be the deciding factor of a loyal fan or a one-time sale.

To make my point that greed or gluttony-styled buyers can have a peaceful side, hasn't there ever been something you chose to save up for? Or perhaps you like buying things only in a certain color? On a minor scale, there's always something some wants or is 'hustling' to obtain. Being a salesperson yourself (I assume because you're reading this book), you know the feeling of wanting to achieve goals without stepping on others, and you're not alone in that mindframe. It's become more of a norm in the last decade.

Allow me to prove the last comment by revealing the other side of this chapter: gluttony. Rather than someone's need to take everything from everyone, instead, what if it's someone looking to improve in a field of study? Now, all they are hungry for is knowledge. Can't be mad at someone for wanting to learn, can you? Well, people who search for knowldge-based products need to be put in this category, because of how you need to approach the sale.

Here is the key about 'glutteny-based buyers'. Someone who falls under the gluttony category is often after a set of some kind. A friend of mine falls under this category (along with him being a 'seer'). I remember when his favorite superhero comic, "The Shadow," came out with five separate covers a couple years ago. Each book told the same story, yet he NEEDED all five different covers. And when I say need, I mean it. At one point he had four out of the five, and when I went to visit him one day he went on for 30 minutes about how he badly he needed the last version. I found this collection very bizarre (then again, I collect different versions of Tolkien's '*The Hobbit,*' so I'm not judging), but he found his craving for this to be normal because it's all he and other fans of 'The Shadow' could talk about. That means, those comic-book writers knew how to capture the market, and worked it well.

These writers help prove my point: make a quality product and people will want to buy it. Maybe even consider lowering the price once and a while for this type of customer and you've created a life-long buyer. And isn't that what all salespeople are after? A dedicated customer base.

Let's use one more example. Say you sell five products that all work together or complement one another. And let's say you price some reasonably at $20. Now, the old rule used to be "pretend like everyone has $20 in their pocket." That still may be the case in some way, but my experience is that if you can get $10 from someone every time they cross your path, they are more likely to tell their friends about you instead of the guy who attempts to suck the $20-life from a one time customer. All this does is make them feel mugged, empty-pocketed, and hesitant to return. Although the term may sound ugly, the gluttonous people are your best friends when it comes to being a dedicated buyer.

Paid With Pride

This could very well be the shortest section in this book. Mainly because when I originally wrote this, "Pride"was going to be fused with "greed." But as more thought went into it, a single difference was screaming at me. Where those were seen as "greed-driven buyers" want for the sake of having it, whether that be a collection, or personal investment, they coul be buying for themselves *or* a friend.

A buyer who is 'Pride-driven' wants to buy only to advance themselves personally. So in many ways, "pride" is a fusion of "greed" and "lust."

Rather then comparing the products to pop-culture in the same manner you would for the 'lustful buyers,' try talking about why this buyer NEEDS IT, personally. Show how it benefits them, and you already have this buyer's interest.

The single difference that separates those who are categorized as "Pride buyers" talk more about themselves more than anything else. So play to that and encourage or complement them. And my personal experience pride people are often "Seers." They won't always be, but it may help you close a lot of the deal quicker while starting off.

Lead By Lust

If the 'Greedy' buyer isn't your common client, this category certainly is. There's an exception to every rule, but more times than not, those who best associate with "lust" are the mainstreamers. These are the people who enjoy what's popular, and 'in'. Hopefully your product is what the people of the fast-paced world find interesting. If not-that's OK-so long as you acknowledge that and make the necessary changes to modernize it, and keep it relevant in your niche.

Don't get stuck on how you think a product should look or what *you* think it should do! This is a hard pill for any entrepreneur or salesman to swallow-but the more mainstream your idea can be-the higher your sales will become. If you believe you know what's best for your customer and try to not only sell your product but you also attempt to sell them on your point of view and life series, you were doing far more harm than good to your business.

However, if you can make your product more mainstream, or at the very least associate your product with something mainstream, you can draw in customers and boost your sales literally overnight!

My first book came out in the middle of the *'Lord Of The Rings: The Hobbit'* film trend. So, I went in search of stores that focused on fantasy novels and stories. When I found these places (and eventually began selling there weekly) I compared my book to the famous trilogy and prequel, but also added that it was "A fresh breath of air for fantasy lovers." Whether my book is on par with 'The Lord of the Rings' is up for debate. The fact of the matter is: I was able to sell enough copies in one day to cover my bills for a whole week. So you make the call-was my book on par with this legendary series? Or did I just know my customers well enough to earn an honest paycheck? Either way, I saw a boost to my income. Something that my bank account greatly think me for. If you can remember to modernize your product while keeping your personal flare attached to it, you will create your own special niche! Speaking of being different than the others, our next topic will definitely be the most unusual of all the personalities.

Paid With Pride

This could very well be the shortest section in this book. Mainly because when I originally wrote this, "Pride"was going to be fused with "greed." But as more thought went into it, a single difference was screaming at me. Where those were seen as "greed-driven buyers" want for the sake of having it, whether that be a collection, or personal investment, they coul be buying for themselves *or* a friend.

A buyer who is 'Pride-driven' wants to buy only to advance themselves personally. So in many ways, "pride" is a fusion of "greed" and "lust."

Rather then comparing the products to pop-culture in the same manner you would for the 'lustful buyers,' try talking about why this buyer NEEDS IT, personally. Show how it benefits them, and you already have this buyer's interest.

The single difference that separates those who are categorized as "Pride buyers" talk more about themselves more than anything else. So play to that and encourage or complement them. And my personal experience pride people are often "Seers." They won't always be, but it may help you close a lot of the deal if you're still starting off in sales.

A Final Note

Now that you have completed this book, you are invited to have a one-on-one with either of the creators of the newest business on style & business motivation, KCX owners Kyle Newton or Colton Boudreau. Not only will they help you set up a S.W.A.T design to help you develop as a salesperson, we will also help you adapt this book to *your* operation of business. From Car dealers to artists, we've helped them all, so why not you? You'll be able to reach out to us by using the email: lostlegendsne@gmail.com. Until we chat, good luck with your next sale, and we look forward to helping you grow!